# THE
# ARMS TRADE

Bernard Harbor & Chris Smith

**ROURKE ENTERPRISES INC.**
Vero Beach, Florida 32964

# World Issues

Endangered Wildlife
Food or Famine?
International Terrorism
Nuclear Weapons
Population Growth
The Arms Trade
The Energy Crisis
The Environment
The International Drug Trade
World Health

**Frontispiece:** A Nicaraguan gunner trains his antiaircraft gun skyward.
**Cover:** Afghan fighters inspect a hand-held rocket launcher.

Text © 1988 Rourke Enterprises Inc.
PO Box 3328, Vero Beach, Florida 32964

Printed in Italy

**Library of Congress Cataloging-in-Publication Data**

Harbor, Bernard, 1960–
    The arms trade/Bernard Harbor.
      p.   cm. – (World issues)
    Bibliography: p.
    Includes index.
    Summary: Discusses the arms trade, how it works, whether it is
sufficiently controlled, and whether there are alternative forms of
trade.
    ISBN 0–86592–283–7
    1. Munitions – Juvenile literature.    [1. Munitions.    2. Arms
control.]    I. Title.    II. Series: World issues (Vero Beach, Fla.)
UF530.H37 1988
382'.456234 – dc19                               88–4537
                                                    CIP
                                                    AC

# Contents

# 1
# Introduction

## The arms trade: why bother?

During World War I soldiers often discovered that they were fighting enemies who were using guns and ammunition produced in their own countries. When Germany invaded Belgium its soldiers faced Belgian troops armed with German guns. When the same army turned east they were met by Soviet troops equipped with German cannons. Throughout this era arms salesmen – the so-called merchants of death – toured the capitals of Europe selling arms to the highest bidders.

> To give arms to all men who offer an honest price for them without respect of persons or principles: to aristocrats and republicans, to Nihilist and Tsar, to Capitalist and Socialist, to Protestant and Catholic, to burglar and policeman, white man and yellow man, to all sorts and conditions, all nationalities, all faiths, all follies, all causes and all crimes.
> *From* Major Barbara *by George Bernard Shaw*

Thankfully, this is no longer the arms trade. A proportion of the trade is still outside, or beneath, government control. Occasionally it goes against national interests but, generally, arms sales are now conducted between governments.

Since 1980, the governments of developing countries have spent approximately $20 billion a year on imported defense equipment. Yet over the same period we have been made acutely aware of poverty in these regions. In parts of Africa there is still famine on a massive scale. In Latin America many countries are faced with huge debts resulting from loans that allowed them to import goods essential for industrial development. Throughout the developing world environmental problems are now posing a threat to human as well as to plant and animal life. It might, therefore, seem strange that developing countries spend so much money on defense and that rich countries seem so willing to sell arms and take money that could be used for clean water, housing and medicine. The reasons why countries buy and sell arms and the effects of the trade are the main points of this book.

**Right** *Map showing the countries that are referred to in this book.*
**Below** *Sir Basil Zaharoff, an international arms dealer, who made huge profits from his dealings during World War I.*

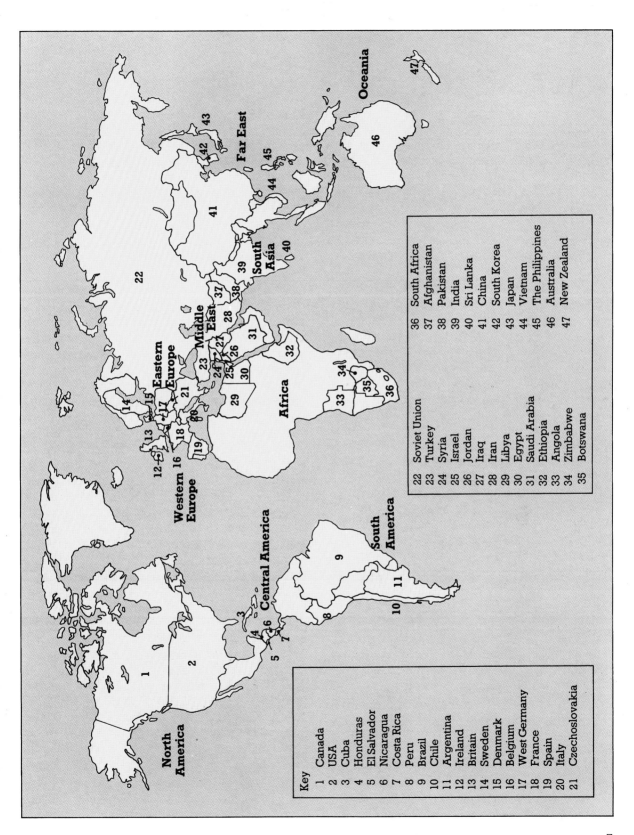

Key
1 Canada
2 USA
3 Cuba
4 Honduras
5 El Salvador
6 Nicaragua
7 Costa Rica
8 Peru
9 Brazil
10 Chile
11 Argentina
12 Ireland
13 Britain
14 Sweden
15 Denmark
16 Belgium
17 West Germany
18 France
19 Spain
20 Italy
21 Czechoslovakia

22 Soviet Union
23 Turkey
24 Syria
25 Israel
26 Jordan
27 Iraq
28 Iran
29 Libya
30 Egypt
31 Saudi Arabia
32 Ethiopia
33 Angola
34 Zimbabwe
35 Botswana

36 South Africa
37 Afghanistan
38 Pakistan
39 India
40 Sri Lanka
41 China
42 South Korea
43 Japan
44 Vietnam
45 The Philippines
46 Australia
47 New Zealand

North America

Central America

South America

Western Europe

Eastern Europe

Middle East

Africa

South Asia

Far East

Oceania

But the arms trade does not just affect people in developing countries. It is an important issue for other reasons too, and in various ways it affects us all.

First, we are interested in the arms trade because it is a major obstacle to a more peaceful world. Selling arms to poor countries may not create wars directly. After all, societies found ways and means of fighting wars long before the invention of the tank, the plane and even the rifle. Nevertheless, by exporting powerful and sophisticated arms to poor countries, which often have more political and territorial problems than, for example, countries in Europe have, there is a risk that these weapons will be used. In the war between Iran and Iraq modern weapons bought before and during the war have sustained a conflict that has cost more than 500,000 lives so far. Since the end of the World War II over 16 million soldiers and civilians have died in wars in the developing world. This is approximately equal to one-quarter of the population of Britain or the whole population of Australia.

Second, we are interested in the arms trade because the act of selling arms tells us a great deal about the countries involved. The international system is a complex arrangement of individual countries. These countries relate to each other through political alliances (such as NATO or ANZUS) and trading arrangements, or through distrust and, sometimes, fear. Moreover, this international system changes continually. Few, if any, countries will sell or give arms to an enemy. Therefore, the act of selling arms tells us much about how countries are getting along with each other.

Third, we are interested in the arms trade because of the jobs that are created when a country that produces arms sells them to other countries. In The United States thousands of jobs are dependent upon continuous arms exports. The same is true for France, the Soviet Union and, to a lesser extent, Britain. Military equipment is very complex to produce and to maintain. From the point when a defense item is no more than an idea or a set of drawings and technical calculations, until the time when the tanks, ships and planes are actually used, jobs are created.

Throughout the developed world unemployment has become a major problem. Trading with other countries is a means of keeping people in work, and the money they earn is used to purchase goods and services that provide work for others. Consequently, if rich countries do not sell arms, a number of people will lose their jobs. However, we must consider whether or not we should regard our own jobs as more important than the other issues we have discussed, particularly as the job losses could probably be compensated by job gains in other areas of trade.

## The arms trade: what is it?

It is important to understand exactly what the arms trade involves. Then we can look in more detail at why countries buy and sell, whether or not there should be more control over arms sales, and whether or not it is possible to find alternative forms of trade. The arms trade is essentially the buying and selling of military technology – the equipment and skills required by a country to defend itself. The trade involves the transfer of resources, ranging from the materials used to build a weapon (steel and aluminum, for example) to the knowledge and information that is necessary to make it work.

We are concerned mainly with major weapons systems such as tanks, ships and planes. These arms make up the bulk of the arms trade because they are so expensive and so important. However, because of their complex nature, they are rarely sold on their own.

Consider, for example, an advanced jet fighter. The pilot must be trained to fly a machine that travels at perhaps twice the speed of sound. He must also be able to use all the weapons on board and identify targets. On the ground, mechanics and technicians must be able to understand and repair the thousands of faults that might occur through stress, malfunction or damage. These days, faults are located by computers, but somebody

*Right* Iranian volunteers on a march before leaving for the war with Iraq. Both sides in this war have imported vast quantities of arms.

must understand and work the computer and then fix the faults that it finds.

Most developing countries, and many relatively rich countries, do not have the ability to do this for themselves. Consequently, along with defense equipment, developing countries import the skills required to operate and maintain weapons. They also import other equipment, such as repair facilities, spare parts and communications systems. Thus, many countries buy their weapons in "packages," but they often do so in the hope that at some time they will be able to build their own weapons.

*Modern weaponry is often extremely complex and requires highly trained crews. This is a system for communicating with ground stations aboard an E-3A AWACS early warning aircraft.*

## The last forty years

Our interest in the arms trade begins in 1945, at the end of World War II. The following years saw many changes in the world political system and the arms trade played an important role.

In 1945 the United States and the Soviet Union emerged from the war as major world powers – superpowers. During the war the countries of Europe had been weakened and their economic and political strength greatly reduced. At the same time, the superpowers had become much stronger. For example, the United States had developed nuclear weapons and the Soviet Union had gained control over several countries in Eastern Europe. The superpowers had many differences that surfaced after the war, and relations between them gradually deteriorated into "Cold War."

*Independence celebrations in Angola, 1975. Since then, Angola has experienced a bitter civil war in which U.S.-backed guerrillas have fought the Soviet-backed government.*

Neither side was prepared to go to war but both were prepared to do anything else that would weaken the other.

Also, in part because the European countries had become so weak, many of their colonies succeeded in winning independence. Consequently, throughout the 1950s and 1960s, new nations emerged in what we now know as the developing world. As these countries became independent they also became responsible for their own defense, and so needed to acquire equipment for this purpose.

In time the competition between the superpowers extended into the developing world. There were two reasons for this. First, many of the new countries had not yet decided where they should fit in the international system. Second, several of these countries bordered the Soviet Union. The U.S. firmly believed that the Soviet Union intended to expand. Consequently, the American government sold at cheap prices, or gave away, large quantities of arms to countries willing to join a system of alliances against the Soviet Union.

Gradually this system lost its effectiveness. The Americans discovered that many of their allies were more interested in acquiring arms than in supporting their mission against the Soviet Union. They also realized that the system was costing them a great deal of money. By the mid-1970s, the U.S. decided that it could no longer afford to give away defense equipment. Instead, it decided that it would sell arms on commercial terms, in a similar fashion to the Western European exporters such as Britain and France.

At about this time, the OPEC (oil-producing) countries raised the price of oil and threw the world economy into confusion. OPEC countries suddenly found themselves with huge cash reserves, which were deposited in Western banks. These banks then lent large amounts to other non-oil-producing countries. Many countries bought arms with the money they borrowed and this resulted in a period of boom for the major arms producers.

In time, as countries completed their defense programs and as their debts to foreign banks rose, they stopped buying arms in such large quantities. Now, the international arms trade is much smaller. Developing countries cannot afford to buy as they did in the 1970s, and the superpowers cannot afford to subsidize their efforts as they did in the 1950s and 1960s. Nevertheless, countries are still buying arms, and in the following chapters we will investigate in more detail why countries buy and sell arms and what can be done to stop, or at least to control, arms sales.

*A 3D electronic scanning radar used by NATO. Very few developing countries could afford such sophisticated defense equipment.*

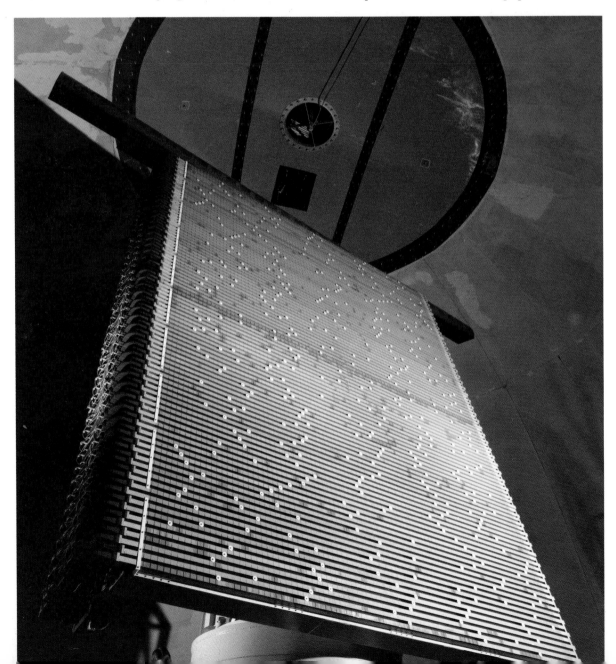

# 2
# Who sells, who buys and how much?

To understand the arms trade, it is necessary to know which countries sell arms and which ones buy. Also it is important to have some idea of how large the trade is. Finding precise information on this, however, is not as easy as it may sound. For example, when Britain announced that it was to sell Tornado fighters to Saudi Arabia in 1985, estimates of the value of the deal ranged from $5 billion to $10 billion. This illustrates the difficulties of measuring and evaluating the arms trade.

A number of problems combine to create these difficulties. Different people and groups use different definitions of an arms sale. This makes it impossible to be sure about what exactly is included in the figures they use. On top of this, the secrecy surrounding military affairs makes it very difficult to collect information.

The figures in this book are the ones used by the Stockholm International Peace Research Institute (SIPRI) in Sweden. They include all major conventional weapons sales: military aircraft, tanks and armored vehicles, artillery, guidance and radar systems, warships and missiles. While this is by no means a perfect definition, it avoids the "gray areas" of the arms trade: things like Land Rovers or computers that could be used for civil as well as military purposes. Also, because major weapons systems are highly visible, it is fairly easy to trace them and to get a better picture of how the arms trade is changing.

## Trends in the arms trade

In the 1970s, the arms trade was labeled "the fastest growing business in the world." A spectacular increase in arms exports occurred for a number of reasons. One was the new wealth of the oil-producing countries, which meant that they had more money to spend on weapons. At the same time, the major arms-exporting countries saw arms sales as a means of getting back some of the large sums that they were

*President Alfonsin of Argentina, elected after the collapse of the military government in 1982, has attempted to reduce his country's defense expenditure.*

now having to spend on oil and other commodities. War and crisis in almost every region of the world stimulated the trade further. Finally, these factors tempted countries to relax their controls on the trade.

The 1980s have, however, seen the end of this boom. The global economic and debt crisis, culminating in the recent drop in prices for oil and other commodities, is the major reason for this. Another is that, as a result of the boom of the 1970s, many developing countries feel that they have plenty of weapons, at least for the time being. Other reasons include an increase in the number of countries that produce arms, and the change from military to civil government that has happened in many developing countries.

All of these factors have contributed to a reduction in the demand for arms, particularly among developing countries and especially in Africa (where the economic crisis is most severe) and South America (where the debt

*Brazilian Tucano aircraft ready for delivery to four South American air forces. Brazil has only recently begun to compete in the international arms market.*

crisis has combined with changes from military to civil government).

At the same time as the demand for arms has declined, the number of suppliers has increased. The boom of the 1970s encouraged traditional arms exporters to sell more weapons rather than to try to sell civil goods. But in recent years, many traditional *importers* of arms have also developed arms industries. Some, like Brazil, have even become successful exporters of weapons.

Twenty years ago the only major arms producers were the United States, the Soviet Union, France, Britain, West Germany and a handful of smaller European countries. Now many more countries can be added. Italy, Spain, Brazil, Israel, China, South Africa and many others are able to make and export weapons. As a result, many more countries are attempting to sell weapons, but fewer countries need to buy them. These two factors have had two major effects.

The first is that the importing country now has more power over the exporter. Because there are plenty of suppliers, all eager to maintain their share of the market, the buyer can now expect to receive the most modern equipment available. There are even examples of

*A Tornado IDS fighter of the Royal Saudi Air Force, Britain's largest-ever export order.*

armies in exporting countries having to use old equipment while the most modern weapons are sold abroad. In the 1970s Britain was selling to Iran more advanced tanks than the British army possessed. Again, in 1985, the British Royal Air Force had to wait for Tornado aircraft while they were sold to Saudi Arabia. And the Soviet Union has sold its most advanced fighter plane, the MiG-29, to India and Zimbabwe.

On top of this, the importer can now expect to share in the production of military equipment and so learn about the advanced technology involved in military production. Also, importers are able to insist that the country that sells them weapons agrees to buy back a certain amount of goods. They can also demand other economic benefits such as good credit terms when they buy arms.

The second effect is that it is becoming more difficult to control the arms trade. Because of their desperation to sell, many countries have relaxed their export restrictions. This allows them to export to more countries, often when

those countries are at war or are guilty of human rights violations. For example, twenty-seven countries have sold weapons to *both* sides in the Iran–Iraq war since it began in 1980.

Some exporting countries have even broken their own laws on selling weapons. Recent examples of this include the United States' covert sale of weapons to Iran at the same time that the U.S. was publicly denouncing Iran for holding American citizens (as well as citizens from other countries) hostage. Another example is the sale of submarine technology by West Germany to South Africa, which is in breach of international law.

> The military export market has shrunk by some 25% in the last couple of years. As a result, the competition between manufacturers (especially in Europe and the developing nations) who must export or become bankrupt is becoming fiercer than every before.
> *Editorial in Swiss journal,* International Defense Review, *June 1987*

## The major exporters

The world arms trade was worth about $160 billion to the exporters between 1982 and 1986. The Soviet Union and the United States are by far the leading arms exporters. They are followed by the major Western European countries (France, Britain, West Germany and Italy) and China (see Figure 1).

Between 1982 and 1986 the **United States** was the world's leading arms exporter, making 34 percent of all arms sales during that period. Just over half of U.S. sales were to the developing world, most of this to the Middle East and the Far East. Most of the remaining U.S. sales were to countries in Western Europe.

Between 1982 and 1986 the **Soviet Union** was the second largest exporter, making just over 30 percent of all sales during that period. Although the U.S. sold more weapons, the Soviet Union was the leading exporter to countries in the developing world. Only about 25 percent of the Soviet exports went to its allies in Eastern Europe. The rest went to developing countries. Its exports to the developing world go to only a few countries. From 1982 to 1986 over 77 percent of Soviet exports to developing countries went to just five countries: Syria, India, Iraq, Libya and Cuba.

Between 1982 and 1986 **Western European countries** accounted for about 25 percent of total world sales of weapons. France has always had a very aggressive sales policy and, as a result, has been Western Europe's leading exporter. Between 1982 and 1986 France accounted for over 12 percent of the global arms trade. In the same period Britain exported 5.5 percent, West Germany 4.4 percent and Italy 2.5 percent of the world total. Since the mid-1970s Britain has been selling more weapons and may now have replaced France as Western Europe's biggest exporter.

Other than the superpowers and Western Europe, the most significant arms exporter is **China**. Between 1982 and 1986 it exported 3.1 percent of the global total. Over 97 percent of this was to developing countries.

**Other developing countries** accounted for 3.3 percent of global exports during the same period. This trade was dominated by a few countries, notably Israel and Brazil and, to a lesser extent, Egypt, Jordan and Libya. Over 95 percent of developing countries' exports were to other developing countries.

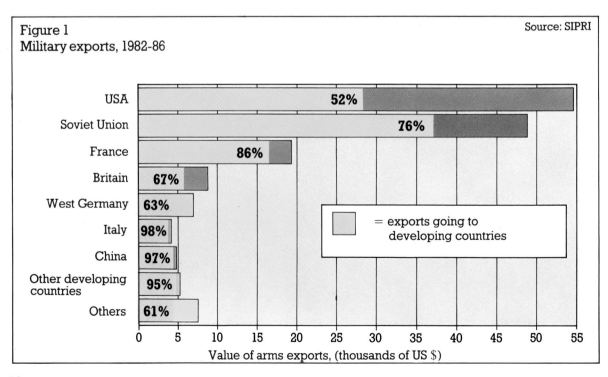

Figure 1
Military exports, 1982-86

Source: SIPRI

= exports going to developing countries

Value of arms exports, (thousands of US $)

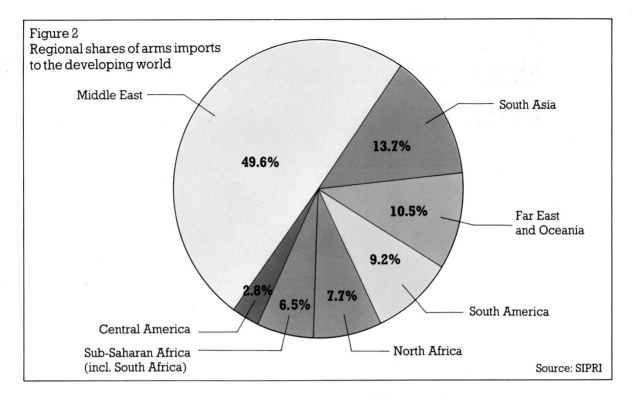

**Figure 2**
Regional shares of arms imports
to the developing world

Middle East — 49.6%

South Asia — 13.7%

Far East and Oceania — 10.5%

9.2%

South America

Central America — 2.8%

6.5%

7.7%

North Africa

Sub-Saharan Africa
(incl. South Africa)

Source: SIPRI

## The major importers

Over the past ten years the developing world's share of arms imports has been around 65–70 percent of the total global trade. The rest has been arms trade within the two main alliances, NATO and the Warsaw Pact. However, it now seems that developing countries are beginning to cut their arms imports.

In some regions imports have remained fairly constant (see Figure 2). The Middle East, with its massive oil wealth, continues to account for around 50 percent of trade to the developing world. Imports to the Far East, though large, have remained steady at about 10 percent of total developing world imports.

However, imports to South Asia have risen dramatically and now account for over 20 percent of the developing world's imports. Most of these go to India and Pakistan. But Latin America and Africa have reduced their arms imports. Both regions have massive debts to pay, and countries there have, on the whole, found it impossible to maintain high levels of arms spending. At the same time, some countries in South America (Argentina, Brazil and Peru) that had previously been ruled by the military now have civil governments. This has helped efforts to reduce spending on arms in those countries. Also, both Brazil and Argentina have developed significant arms industries of their own. So, between 1982 and 1986 Latin America imported about 12 percent of developing countries' arms imports while Africa imported just over 14 percent.

## What about the future?

The recent drop in demand for weapons has caused many changes in the pattern of the arms trade. The economic reasons for the lack of demand (such as the drop in oil prices and the massive debts of many developing countries) suggest that there will never again be a boom similar to that of the 1970s. But the last two decades have shown how unpredictable the arms trade is. It is, therefore, hard to make any forecasts about the future. However, it seems likely that the difficulties of trying to find customers in the modern arms market will continue to make it more and more difficult to control the arms trade.

# 3
# Why sell arms?

As we have seen, it is becoming increasingly difficult to sell arms. So why do countries put so much effort into it? Different countries have different reasons for selling arms and these often change. However, the reasons given for selling weapons fall into two broad groups: political and national security reasons, and economic reasons.

Sometimes there will be a conflict between these considerations, and a country may then have to give up the economic benefits of selling arms because of political factors. For example, the United States has been unable to sell a lot of very advanced weapons to Saudi Arabia and other countries in the Middle East. This is not because those countries do not want to buy the weapons. Rather, it is because they are hostile to Israel, and recent administrations in the U.S. have been pro-Israeli.

Generally, a nation's policy on arms sales will be motivated by a blend of political and economic reasons rather than by one or the other. These pressures to sell arms will combine rather than conflict, and will create a powerful incentive to maintain and expand arms sales.

> We certainly are in a hell of a business when a fellow has to wish for trouble so as to make a living.
>
> *Frank S. Jonas, military sales agent*

*The U.S. government is eager to extend its political influence in Central American countries. Here, an American military adviser is training Honduran soldiers.*

## Political reasons

Many countries are anxious to sell as many weapons as they can. But at the same time they are very careful about their choice of customer. This is because they have to take care that arms sales do not harm their national security or foreign policy interests. Indeed, if it is possible, exporters want to use arms exports to improve their security and further their foreign policy interests.

The main political benefit that exporting nations hope to gain from selling arms is the extension of their influence to other countries and regions. Since the end of World War II it has been common for countries to sell weapons, or even give them away, to make other

*These Iranian Air Force Tomcats are virtually useless because the U.S. will no longer sell spare parts to the hostile Iranian government.*

countries friendly toward them.

The importer of weapons is friendly to the exporter because it does not want to do anything to upset or threaten its supplier. If it did, it would risk losing its supply of arms. Also, it would risk losing access to all of the spare parts that are needed to keep modern weapons going. These days, weapons are made up of thousands of fragile and sophisticated "high-tech" parts, some of which are bound to go wrong. If importing countries are not able to buy spare parts from the exporters, the weapons can soon become useless.

Therefore, the supplier can influence the policies of the importer. For instance, it can expect political and military support when it needs it. In this way the United States is able to maintain naval bases in the Philippines, and the Soviet Union can maintain a large naval base in Vietnam. The supplier can also expect access to the raw materials and other products of the importer. For example, Western countries guarantee their oil supplies by selling weapons to countries in the Middle East. Equally important, from the supplier's point of view, is the ability to prevent its enemies from exerting a similar influence.

In times of war, an exporting nation will often supply weapons to the side that it wants to see win. This might be because that country is an ally of the exporter or because it is at war with an enemy of the exporter. Sometimes it may just be that the exporter thinks that it will benefit more from the defeat of one country than another.

There are countless examples of this. The United States supplies weapons to the *Contra* forces fighting the Nicaraguan government in Central America because it wants to see a change of government in that country. The Soviet Union supplies weapons to the governments of countries like Nicaragua, Angola and Ethiopia that are engaged in wars or conflicts because it wants them to survive.

But exporting nations also sell weapons to friendly or allied nations when they are not at war as a way of enhancing their own national security. For example, it is important to the United States that its European allies in NATO are able to repel a potential Soviet invasion. Similarly, the Soviet Union wants its allies in Eastern Europe to have well-equipped armed forces so that its own security is not threatened.

A supplier may also think it important that a military balance is maintained in certain geographical regions. If it sees its enemies gaining influence in a region, it may supply arms to other countries in the area in order to alter the balance. For example, the Soviet Union supplies Syria with weapons to counter American influence in the Middle East.

The amount of influence that can be exerted by the supplier will be affected by a number of things, but particularly by the ability and willingness of other countries to supply arms. We have seen that the number of countries attempting to export weapons is growing. This makes it more difficult to sell arms, which, in turn, improves the bargaining position of the buyer and reduces the amount of influence that can be gained by the exporter.

*An American military base in the Philippines. The United States regards these bases as vital to its security interests in the Pacific.*

*The Nicaraguan army is equipped largely with Soviet arms. Some Americans fear that the Soviets are using Nicaragua to gain a political "foothold" in Central America.*

## Economic reasons

Weapons are not made by countries but by companies. Companies manufacture and sell weapons in order to make a profit. Sometimes, after all of their costs have been met (wages, rent, equipment, and so on) companies have little profit left. But, on the whole, they will make more profit if they can sell more weapons. For this reason most armament companies will try to sell to as many countries as possible.

As we have seen, governments may have

> If we decline to accept an order . . . we know that other countries . . . will accept the same order.
>
> *Chairperson of a British arms-exporting company, quoted in* Morals and Missiles *(British Parliamentary Human Rights Group, 1980)*

reasons to prevent companies from selling arms to certain other countries even though this may be profitable. But they also have economic reasons for encouraging arms exporters. These fall into four main areas: improving the balance of payments, employing more people, reducing the cost of weapons, and gaining access to raw materials and to other trade.

21

It is difficult to make a precise assessment of the contribution arms sales make to the balance of payments of any country, but most exporting nations say that this is one of the major benefits of overseas sales. Much was made of this after the huge increases in the price of oil and other raw materials in the early 1970s. Arms sales to the newly rich Middle Eastern countries were seen as a way of recovering some of the vast sums of money that Western nations were now having to spend on oil. It has been estimated, for example, that France has been able to cover about one-fifth of its oil bills by selling arms.

Most major arms exporters say that selling arms to other countries helps to create jobs. The more weapons that are sold (at home or abroad), the more people that are needed to develop and manufacture them. The Boeing Corporation, maker of the 747 and other commercial planes, wins many government contracts for defense and aerospace projects. Boeing is also America's second leading exporter, with

> In Europe there is an arms industry that must be kept going. What are they supposed to do with their goods? Naturally, export them to powers at war.
> *Karl-Erik Schmitz, arms salesman*

sales to many other countries. When Boeing's business is slow, towns in which its factories are located suffer economically.

Areas that rely on industries dominated by military production prosper during wars and suffer during peacetime. But why don't governments help these industries focus on the production of civil goods for exports and jobs rather than rely on the increasingly difficult military market?

*In times of high unemployment, governments are reluctant to curb arms exports because of the fear that this could put jobs at risk.*

Most of the major industrial nations think it necessary to maintain the ability to produce at least some of their own military equipment. This is because they do not want to be dependent on foreign suppliers for their national security needs. They feel that it is important that they are prepared for any wars that might break out. Many think that being able to make weapons in their own country is a vital part of this preparation. In order to be able to do this, governments must protect their arms industries and make sure that they stay in business.

However, modern military technology is becoming more and more expensive. For example, it is 320 times more expensive to make a modern American F-111 aircraft than it was to make the F-5 during World War II. Most governments are therefore finding it harder to pay for their weapons. Increasingly, they look to exports to help bear the burden

*American military personnel examine armored vehicles and other equipment at a French armaments exhibition.*

of the huge cost of modern weapons. Exports can do this because the countries that buy the arms pay some of the cost of designing and manufacturing them. Also, it becomes cheaper to produce weapons if greater numbers of them are made.

Finally, it is widely believed that exporting weapons creates a good climate for further trade. An exporter can expect to gain access both to the products of the recipient nation and to other markets in that country or region. This may take the form of direct barter of arms for other goods (such as arms-for-oil deals that have become fairly common since the late 1970s) or the creation of good political relationships that encourage further trade.

Arms exports do offer economic benefits in all of these areas, but there are two sides to every coin. The arms market is already volatile. This means that changes can occur suddenly and without warning. There are many examples of export orders being canceled because of a change in the international situation.

As the arms market becomes more and more competitive, it is becoming less certain that any given nation, industry or company will be able to maintain its overseas sales. In the light of this it seems more and more risky to rely on the arms market to maintain a healthy balance of payments or to maintain employment. Perhaps it would be wiser to encourage the development of civil industries to do these things. Also, the extent to which exports can help to reduce the cost of maintaining arms industries has never been fully proved.

The use of arms sales as a tool of foreign policy has often proved to be a double-edged sword. A military coup, revolution or other change of government can transform an ally into an adversary. Following the Iranian revolution in 1979 the new regime was particularly hostile to the U.S. and Britain, both of whom had supplied the former government with modern weaponry. Again, in today's volatile market, the political benefits to be gained from selling weapons are becoming less certain.

Finally, when weighing the benefits and penalties of exporting arms, it is impossible to avoid the moral questions involved. Who is receiving the weapons and what are they being used for? Couldn't the money being spent on arms imports be spent on food, health, education and other more important things? Before examining these questions in more detail it is necessary to look at the reasons why nations import weapons.

*The British warship HMS* Sheffield *was hit by an Exocet missile during the Falklands War with Argentina. Britain supplied parts for the missile to the manufacturer in France, who sold the missile to Argentina.*

# 4
# Why buy arms?

All countries have to be able to defend themselves. The terms defense and security, however, lack precise meaning. True security is a state of being, a feeling of freedom from fear. It cannot be measured by quantities of weapons, conventional or nuclear. The United States has far more weapons in its arsenal than France, for instance, but probably feels no more secure.

Countries import arms for a number of reasons. Most of these relate in some way to the problem of insecurity. First, governments have a duty to protect their citizens and the territory they inhabit. To achieve this, each country should have clearly defined borders that everybody agrees upon and respects, and no other country should violate those borders. Second, governments must protect their economies, including raw materials and industry. Third, some countries buy certain types of arms for the prestige they bring. Quite simply, they want to "keep up with the Joneses."

## Security

Nobody likes to feel insecure. The need for security is one of the most basic human instincts. As individuals, we all spend a considerable part of our daily life attempting to find security. This is why we buy houses, save money and contribute to pension plans. Also, we tend to seek security in groups. The family makes us feel secure, particularly in developing countries with no welfare states.

At a different level, governments are responsible for national security. In theory (but hardly ever in practice) the United Nations looks after the security of nations by resolving political differences that might lead to war. Also, the United Nations attempts to persuade countries to adopt policies that will lead to disarmament.

Throughout European history there have been many wars. European nations, as we know them today, were created from centuries of wars culminating in the two World Wars. Since 1945 Europe has avoided war between nations, but this is unusual. The reasons are chiefly that most countries now agree about where borders should be, and, as a continent, Europe has discovered ways of communicating

*The Potsdam Conference in 1945 determined the map of postwar Europe. Sitting (l to r): British Prime Minister Clement Attlee, American President Harry Truman, and the Russian leader Joseph Stalin.*

and managing disputes without resorting to armed conflict. Governments now feel that the terrible cost of war is greater than the economic and political benefits that might result from it. However, this may not always be the case. And even in Europe, the Basques in Spain and the IRA in Northern Ireland are fighting in support of separatist claims.

In the developing world there are still many territorial, political and religious disputes. When European countries such as France, Britain, Portugal, Spain and Italy took over vast areas of land in Africa and Asia there were no countries as we know them today – there were empires and chiefdoms, for example. When the territories became too big to handle as one unit, such as in Africa, they were divided up by administrators who looked at the problem as an urban planner might look at a street system. The result may have looked efficient from a distance (a political map of Northern Africa is full of straight lines), but there was often little consideration of the people who lived inside the boundaries.

*Fighters of the Irish Republican Army (IRA) in Northern Ireland, armed with Soviet rocket launchers, lie in wait for a British army patrol.*

Consequently, when these countries became independent, they inherited boundaries that had been established for administrative reasons and little more. Some thought that their boundaries should be increased. Other countries found themselves with large groups of citizens who, for religious or ethnic reasons, did not quite fit in with the rest of the population. Some groups found themselves split, half in one country and half in another. The situation was very unsatisfactory, but, despite this mess, the new governments had to maintain security.

Sorting out the territorial problems became a major problem in the developing countries and led to many conflicts and wars. Israel fought to defend its right to exist, although this meant that the Palestinian people lost their homeland. India and China fought a bitter border war in 1962, and their differences are still unresolved. Nor could India reach any form of agreement with Pakistan over which country should control the northern state of Kashmir.

Also, since independence many developing countries have experienced civil wars and separatist movements. South Asia, India, Pakistan and Sri Lanka have all experienced at one time or another ethnic disturbances and separatist claims resulting in violence and loss of life. Much the same is true of Southwest Asia where the Kurds in Turkey, Iran and Iraq have fought for a separate state.

To add to this confusion and uncertainty, the

> ... The Third World are grown up people; they have real problems, they have real conflicts. And to regard them as simply the puppets of arms manufacturers is, frankly ... insulting to them.
> *Michael Howard being interviewed by the Canadian journal,* Peace and Security, *1987*

> ... Surely Iran and Iraq couldn't have been pounding each other for seven years except that there are so many Western arms on the market.
> *Journalist*

Cold War between the two superpowers spread to the developing world. Pressure was placed upon the newly independent countries to join alliances, make choices between communist and capitalist systems and accept military, economic and technical aid. This often amounted to little more than a system of bribery and coercion.

Other problems emerged as a direct result of the Cold War. Since World War II the superpowers have often become involved in the internal affairs of developing countries. On occasions their action has been direct. After the revolution in Cuba, the United States launched the Bay of Pigs invasion in an unsuccessful attempt to unseat Fidel Castro. The U.S. also became involved in a long and painful war in Vietnam – a conflict that cost billions of dollars and hundreds of thousands of lives.

When Czechoslovakia decided to experiment with a more liberal form of government in 1968, it was invaded by the Soviet Union. The Soviet Union also propped up the awful regime of Idi Amin in Uganda, has sup-

*In this Palestinian refugee camp in Lebanon even the children are armed and trained to fight.*

*The armed struggle between the Soviet Union and Afghan guerrillas has led to an exodus of millions of refugees from Afghanistan to camps like this in Pakistan.*

ported the exploits of Colonel Qaddafi in Libya and invaded Afghanistan in 1979 when the Marxist government there came under threat.

The rights and wrongs of these cases are very difficult to sort out. Many of the examples used here have led to suffering on the part of small, weak countries and ethnic minorities. Nevertheless, as George Orwell once remarked, the oppressed are not always in the right. The world is too complicated for that. There is a great deal of truth in the observation that one person's "terrorist" is another person's "freedom fighter."

These are some of the reasons why countries buy arms when they cannot produce defense equipment themselves. They must protect themselves against aggression from countries with whom they have disagreements, including, perhaps, one of the superpowers. Governments must also consider the internal aspects of security and be able to protect their citizens from violent groups, perhaps with separatist claims, inside their countries. Unfortunately, internal security is often used by governments as an excuse for brutal and unjust acts of repression against their legitimate opponents.

## Development

Some developing countries are fortunate enough to possess valuable raw materials such as uranium or oil, which can make them wealthy. However, they can also increase security problems by giving enemies a reason for invasion or other hostile actions. The United States has frequently said that it will consider using force in the Middle East if political events mean that it can no longer acquire adequate oil supplies.

Also, some countries have invested heavily in their industries and this investment must be protected along with people and raw materials. Governments in developing countries often argue that development is pointless unless it is protected. This argument is sometimes used as an emotive way of gaining support for large defense programs.

## Keeping up with the Joneses

In many cases, countries buy arms because of threats to their security. In other instances, they buy weapons, or attempt to produce them, because they think it will make their country appear more powerful and important.

The last Shah of Iran, who was overthrown by the Ayatollah Khomeini, was alleged to have had the habit of leafing through defense magazines and choosing equipment on the basis of glossy advertisements. However, decisions about defense are usually made by a number of people – members of defense staffs, civil servants and politicians. When advanced-weapons systems are seen to increase a country's status, it is often in the interests of all the decision-makers to vote in favor of buying them, even when there are no strong military arguments for doing so.

In seeking to raise their prestige, countries tend to buy conspicuous weapons that give the appearance of strength. India has bought two aircraft carriers and wants two more for this precise reason. It also exploded a nuclear "device" in 1974, although after the test it decided not to build nuclear weapons.

After their defeat in World War II, Japan and West Germany were prevented from developing full military strength. A few countries have decided not to compete in military terms at all. Costa Rica has even disbanded its army. However, most countries view an army, navy and air force as important symbols of their independence, like capital cities, universities and national airlines. Even if international prestige were not valued so highly, and more countries decided to do what Costa Rica has done, this would not entirely rule out the need to buy arms from overseas. However, it could alter the type of arms that are bought and, as the high-prestige weapons are usually the most expensive, it could reduce the amount of money spent on defense.

*High-ranking military officers often occupy a privileged and influential position in the societies of developing countries.*

# 5 The effects of the arms trade

## Effects on the importing country

Economic development was once considered to be inevitable and little more than a question of good planning and hard work. For various reasons (not least the fact that many countries have done both and still remain poor) we are no longer convinced that this is true. Poor countries have been unable to improve the lives of most of their citizens. The basic facilities that are taken for granted in rich countries, such as clean water, food, shelter and basic health care, are still not widely available in many developing countries. As a result, other explanations have emerged to explain underdevelopment. One of the most powerful explanations centers around the idea of "dependency." Poor countries, it is argued, stay poor because it is in the political and economic interests of the rich countries to keep them that way.

At the same time, there has been a great deal of interest in the amount of money that developing countries spend on defense. This, too, has become linked to the idea that rich countries benefit from the continuing poverty of the developing world.

Weapons, and all the technology that is required to use them efficiently, cost enormous sums of money. The Mirage 2000, an advanced fighter-bomber produced and sold by the French, costs about $35 million. India has recently bought a second-hand aircraft carrier from Britain for over $90 million. An Exocet guided missile costs more than $100,000.

If poor countries buy arms from foreign sources, they are almost always required to pay in foreign exchange, that is in the currencies of developed countries, such as dollars, sterling or yen. This also applies to the purchase of technology or expertise for development purposes. Consequently, the earning of foreign exchange is very important for development. Some foreign exchange comes in the form of economic aid from the rich countries. However, very often aid is given on the strict condition that it is spent on certain types of goods from the donor country.

Foreign exchange can also be earned in other ways. Citizens working outside the country may send back foreign exchange for relatives or for investment. Although the individual amounts are usually small, the overall sum may be large. Developing countries may have natural resources that can be sold on the international market. If they are scarce, and if there are few substitutes, large amounts of foreign exchange can be earned. Developing countries may have an environment and a climate suited to growing products not easily grown elsewhere, such as coffee or tropical fruits, which sell well in rich countries. Plentiful labor and low wages may encourage the growing of crops that can be exported at low prices, or the development of light manufacturing or assembly industries. For example, many countries in the Far East earn foreign exchange by producing electronic goods.

**Right** *A tea-picker in Kenya. Cash crops like tea earn foreign exchange, but take land away from local food production.*

But it is not easy to earn foreign exchange. The international market is very competitive. Rich countries do not like to see poor countries undercut the prices of their own products. Inflation in the West means that poor countries can buy fewer and fewer industrial goods for their foreign exchange. In other words, they have to export more to import the same. Above all, however, foreign exchange is often earned at great human cost. Farm workers and factory workers are paid very low wages, work long hours and both live and work in very poor conditions. There are too few jobs available, so people are prepared to compete for jobs that pay less than a living wage. In many countries, trade unions are forbidden, social security is unknown and governments permit the exploitation of men, women and children.

*Street-dwellers in Calcutta, India. Despite widespread poverty, India spends huge sums on weapons.*

*Riot police attack demonstrators in Chile. The Chilean army is used by the government to repress its domestic opponents.*

Over the past twenty years more and more foreign exchange has been spent on increasingly expensive defense equipment. However, buying weapons does not add to a country's development efforts. Certainly, every country must spend a certain amount on defense, but the present situation in developing countries is that many are spending much more than they can afford. The victims of this situation are the very poor. If governments were to spend less on defense, they could choose to spend more on health programs, famine relief, education and agriculture. Also, governments could buy more industrial equipment, which would have the effect of providing jobs and reducing imports

> The neglect of social needs in the pursuit of military power has left one person in five in grinding poverty.
> *Ruth Sivard,* World Military and Social Expenditures, *1986*

of manufactured goods, thus saving foreign exchange.

Many governments that spend lavishly on weapons are also very repressive. Consequently, arms imports are often used to repress trade unions, minority rights organizations, civil liberty groups and others. To a certain extent, therefore, the arms trade can be directly related not just to economic underdevelopment but also to political repression and the abuse of human rights.

> Military-controlled governments are more than twice as likely as other Third World governments to make frequent use of torture and other forms of violent repression.
> *Ruth Sivard*, World Military and Social Expenditures, *1986*

If developing countries were to stop importing expensive weapons and reduce their military spending, this would not automatically lead to development. Over the past few years we have seen an overall reduction in military expenditure in the developing world, but there has been little progress on development and still less on human rights. However, substantial cuts would open up new opportunities for development. At present, developing countries argue that this might be true, but that their external and internal security situations give them no choice but to maintain well-equipped defense forces.

### Effects on the exporting country

Chapter 3 outlined the economic reasons for selling arms. But there are also economic disadvantages to selling weapons abroad. Many of these reasons apply to *all* military production, even if it is for the producer's armed forces rather than for export. But some apply specifically to arms exports.

The first is that arms export contracts are sometimes canceled very suddenly. Exporters are jubilant when they win large export orders.

But arms exports are affected more by international politics than are most other exports. Because of this, changes in the international situation can sometimes lead to the cancellation of orders. All of the benefits that come from arms exports are then lost as well. The major example of this in recent years was the cancellation of large orders for American and British military equipment following the Iranian revolution in 1979.

Now that it is so much more difficult to compete in the arms market, the economic benefits of exporting weapons are becoming much less obvious. Because it is so difficult to sell weapons, buyers now demand, and receive, all kinds of economic inducements from exporters. These can reduce the benefits of selling weapons quite a lot.

Importers may demand to be taught about the technology involved in arms production. This means that in the future the buyer may be able to make its own military equipment and so the exporter will have lost part of its market. For example, Brazil, which once imported many weapons, now has an arms industry of its own. It is able to make many of its own weapons and sells many to other countries.

Sometimes importers demand that the exporter buys goods from them worth as much, or more, than the value of the arms deal. When this happens the balance of payments advantages of selling weapons are lost. Indeed, the deal may even harm the balance of payments. Such an arrangement means that few or no jobs are created in the exporting country. Jobs may even be lost if the goods bought from the arms importer replace those already made in the exporting country.

### The costs of military production

Like any other form of government spending, money spent on military production has some positive effects. People have to be employed to make weapons, so jobs and wealth are created. In turn, these people spend their money on other goods and services, so more jobs and wealth are created.

However, evidence shows that since World War II those countries that have devoted a lot of resources to military production (like the

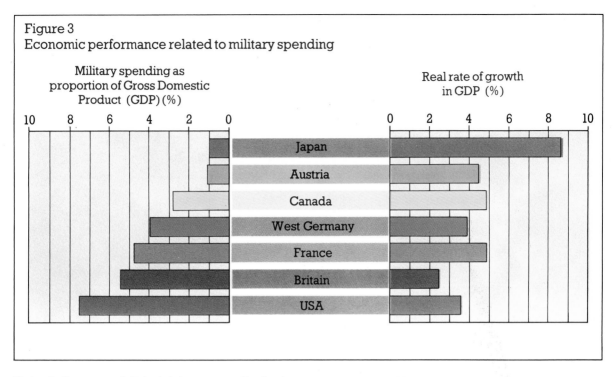

Figure 3
Economic performance related to military spending

Military spending as proportion of Gross Domestic Product (GDP) (%)

Real rate of growth in GDP (%)

United States and Britain) have usually had a worse economic performance than those (like Japan and West Germany) who spend much less (see Figure 3).

It has also been found that, although money spent on military production helps to create jobs, more jobs can be created by government spending on health, education, construction, or most other forms of government spending (see Figure 4).

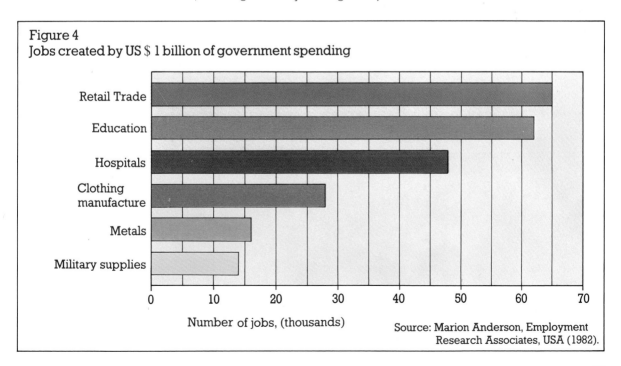

Figure 4
Jobs created by US $ 1 billion of government spending

Number of jobs, (thousands)

Source: Marion Anderson, Employment Research Associates, USA (1982).

The most damaging effect that military production has on economic performance, however, is that it diverts scientists and engineers from inventing and developing civil goods. Because so much effort goes into military production, many countries find that they do not have enough skilled people left to develop other products. This means that while they are trying to sell in the difficult military market, they cannot compete in civil markets because their civil products are not good enough.

This is rather like a student spending all of his or her time preparing for a mathematics examination while ignoring all other studies. Although he or she may be at the top of the class in mathematics, the student may be at the bottom of the class in most other subjects.

Because military technology is extremely specialized, it is difficult to find other uses for it. So, if countries use up a lot of their resources on making weapons, they lag behind in other areas. This problem is made worse by the

*The skills used by scientists and engineers to develop weapons are often the same ones that could be used to make civil products.*

difficulty of catching up technologically once others have progressed. This is especially true these days when technological changes occur so rapidly.

Obviously there are economic benefits to be reaped from making weapons and selling them abroad. But there are as many, if not more, to be had from making other things. Arms exporters could certainly benefit from a reduction in the arms trade if they were to devote their resources to making other goods.

Therefore, controlling the arms trade could be good for the economies of arms exporters as well as having beneficial effects in the importing countries. The next chapter looks at some of the efforts that have been made to control the arms trade and at why it has proved so difficult to do so effectively.

# 6 Controlling the arms trade

## Past attempts at control

There have been several attempts to control the arms trade this century. The first came after World War I when the League of Nations (the forerunner to the United Nations) was appalled by the terrible loss of life in the war and by the partial responsibility of the arms suppliers. As a result, the League attempted to persuade countries to make a register of the arms they were buying and selling. These efforts failed. Countries were simply not interested in cooperating. Before they had a chance to propose another idea, the League itself collapsed. It was eventually replaced by the United Nations, but not until after World War II. In the 1930s all European countries were either making or buying a lot of weapons in preparation for a possible war, which eventually started in 1939. During this period any form of control was seen as a disadvantage.

After World War II the arms trade became a major aspect of international politics. Consequently, it became a concern for the newly established United Nations. But it was not until 1965 that the first initiative was taken. Malta, a country involved in neither buying nor selling of arms, asked the Eighteen Nation Disarmament Committee (which is now the Conference on Disarmament) to consider the arms trade. The Committee made an attempt to monitor the trade, but soon discovered that the superpowers were not interested in declaring what they were selling or giving away.

The importers were also opposed to the initiative because the proposals seemed to discriminate against them. They demanded that if imports were to be registered then so should arms production. Efforts by Denmark in 1967 and Sweden and Britain in 1970 to establish an arms trade register failed for the same reasons.

*Britain's Lord Fenner Brockway, who has long campaigned for disarmament, speaking on the subject at the age of ninety-three.*

A second approach from within the United Nations came from its attempts to link disarmament and development. This approach was seen as a means of closing the gap between developed and developing countries.

In 1950, therefore, the General Assembly issued a resolution stating that the United Nations was determined to "reduce to a minimum the diversion for armament of its human and economic resources and to strive toward the development of such resources for the general welfare, with due regard to the needs of the underdeveloped areas of the world." This was followed by several proposals from a range of countries (India, Brazil, France, the Soviet Union) to establish a fund that would hold all the money saved through disarmament in the North. This would then be spent on worthwhile development projects in the South. The reduction of military expenditure and disarmament in developing countries was not at that time seen to be a major problem.

*A U.N. Special Session on Disarmament, 1982. Despite a number of initiatives, U.N. attempts to promote disarmament have had little effect.*

The world can either continue to pursue the arms race with characteristic vigor, or it can move consciously and with deliberate speed toward a more sustainable economic and political order. *It cannot do both* ... The arms race and underdevelopment are not two problems: they are one. They must be solved together or neither will ever be solved.
*Inga Thorsson, Chairperson of United Nations Group of Government Experts on the Relationship between Disarmament and Development, 1981*

Efforts to link disarmament and development failed almost as badly as the efforts to halt the arms trade. Not surprisingly, other efforts outside the United Nations also failed. Perhaps the most ambitious of all the efforts on the part of individual countries to control arms sales was the attempt by the United States to reach an agreement with the Soviet Union on the control of arms sales to developing countries.

When the Americans elected President Carter in 1976, he promised that foreign policy would show a respect for human rights and development. In the early days of his presidency, Carter did many things to improve American foreign policy. He established a human rights office to monitor the human rights records of countries with whom the U.S. had ties. He also restricted the sale of American military technology to developing countries.

In addition to his efforts to reach a second strategic arms limitation agreement (SALT II), Carter's most ambitious project was the attempt to reach a Conventional Arms Sales Treaty with the Soviet Union. Talks were opened in 1977, and for the first few weeks it seemed as though some form of agreement would be reached. However, the talks eventually failed, largely because overall relations between the two superpowers became much worse during the late 1970s.

*Improved relations between the Soviet Union and the U.S. during President Carter's term raised hopes of progress on disarmament.*

In 1977 the United Nations placed an arms embargo upon South Africa in response to the *apartheid* system. This has been much more successful than other attempts to control the arms trade. In theory, all countries are now prevented from selling arms to South Africa. However, the U.N. has no real power to do anything to stop countries that do not accept the embargo. France and Israel still sell military technology to South Africa, and there is still a great deal of confusion over what can and cannot be sold and what constitutes defense equipment. For example, how should the U.N. classify a very sophisticated computer that might be bought for monitoring the weather but could also be used for acquiring information on troop movements in neighboring countries?

Some countries, such as Sweden, have adopted policies that prevent the sale of arms to countries or regions where there is a risk of war. This is called a "restrictive" policy. However, there are very few countries who manage to maintain this type of policy. Sometimes the pressures on companies and countries to sell arms for profit are just too great, and restrictive policies are ignored. Recently, the Swedish defense company Bofors has come under great criticism for selling arms to the Middle East via Singapore. The Middle East is a region embargoed by the Swedish government. The same company has also been accused of bribing members of the Indian government in order to sell a very large number of field guns.

*An artillery piece made by the Swedish company Bofors. It was revealed in Inida in 1987 that the company had paid 250 million kronas in bribes to Indian government officials.*

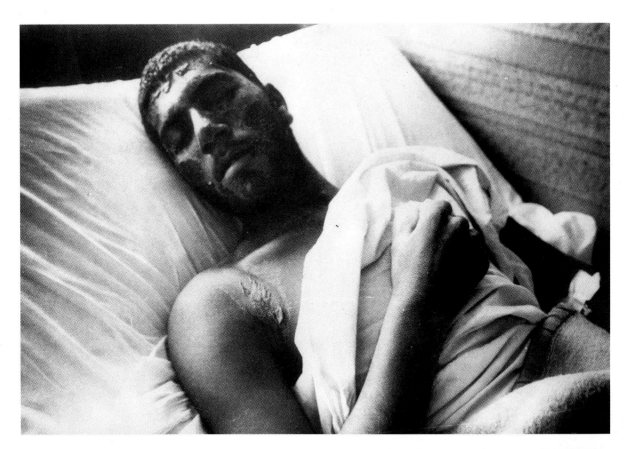

*An Iranian victim of Iraqi chemical weapons. Several companies in the U.S. and Europe have been found to be secretly supplying Iraq with the chemicals to make these dreadful weapons.*

## The problems of control

Without doubt, the failure to control or stop the flow of arms to the developing world is due mainly to the fact that both exporters and importers want the arms trade to continue. Neither side sees that there is anything to gain from a system of control. Both agree that there is much to lose. For the sellers there is a concern that they may be prevented from making sales and profits. The buyers worry that during times of war or periods of tension they could be left without the means to defend themselves, particularly if they cannot produce arms. So, the failure to control the arms trade is basically the result of a lack of political will on the part of all the countries involved.

Even if the will were present, controlling the

> It is almost a perpetual motion machine. We all agree that the arms race is a disaster ... The old problem is, who is going to take the first move to really pull back?
>
> *Sam Cummings, arms salesman*

arms trade would not be easy. There is a large market in covert, or concealed, arms sales. In 1986, for example, the United States secretly sold arms to Iran. This is an example of how easy it is for countries to break the rules of the game. Obviously, we have no idea how much of the arms trade is concealed, but there is general agreement that covert arms sales are on the increase. It is difficult to conceal the sale of tanks or aircraft, but it is much easier to sell rifles or missiles without attracting attention. So, even if countries were interested in controlling arms sales, they would first have to deal with covert arms sale.

*This trawler was captured in 1984 with a cargo of 7 tons of weapons en route from the United States to Ireland.*

The concealed arms trade frequently involves governments. However, private arms dealers are often concerned too. The web of private arms dealers is very complex. It involves fake companies and other fronts, large amounts of money and very secretive dealings. London is often said to be the center for this kind of business. How much governments know about this trade is uncertain, but it is probably more than they admit. In any case, it is very difficult to control. There are also registered private arms dealers who buy and sell second-hand equipment quite legally and openly. However, few governments see it as in their interests to allow this side of the trade to increase beyond a certain limit.

Even if countries could reach some form of international agreement over controlling the flow of arms from developed to developing countries, it would be extremely difficult to put into practice. Under the present system there are too many channels open for concealed arms sales, and these would certainly increase if restrictions were imposed.

# 7 Conclusions

The arms trade is a very complicated issue. It is linked to almost every important question that the world faces.

First, it has to do with security, defense and disarmament. Are weapons necessary at all? If so, how many weapons does a country need to be safe from attack? What kinds of weapons are needed and where can countries get them? Can controlling the arms trade help to bring about disarmament and improve the prospects for world peace?

The arms trade also raises questions about development. Almost everyone wants to see an end to poverty. But is this possible when even the poorest countries spend so much money on arms?

The pattern of the arms trade – who sells to whom – also tells us a lot about relationships between the different countries of the world, including the relations of the superpowers with other countries and with each other. This, then, links up with the important questions of nuclear weapons and nuclear disarmament.

As well as giving us information about the defense and foreign policies of exporting and importing countries, the arms trade also tells us about the domestic economic policies and problems of the exporting countries. For example, it is because many Western economies are in decline that the jobs preserved by arms exports are guarded so jealously.

Because it links all of these issues, the arms trade is both interesting and important. But it also means that studying the arms trade is very difficult because so many things have to be taken into consideration before the trade can be properly understood. If we want to change the arms trade in any way, we have to have some understanding of the interaction of all of these things.

The harmful effects of the trade (the cost of weapons, their use in wars, and so on) suggest that most people would want to stop it. However, it is obvious that many people, in both the exporting and importing countries, want to see it continue.

> The values and principles we live by as a nation will be what history will remember America for, not the sophistication or quantity of our weapons.
> *Senate Report on Arms to Iran, 1986*

Can we conclude that it is impossible to control the arms trade? Under the present system the answer is probably yes; the arms trade cannot be controlled, no matter how beneficial this would be for developing countries. The only possibility for controlling and reducing the amount of arms sold to developing countries is through changes in the international system. This could happen in one of two ways. The system could mature to a point where arms are needed less than they are now or not at all. This is unlikely, however much we might wish for a more peaceful world. Alternatively, developing countries could attempt to design new defense policies that do not rely so much on the most expensive technology available. Already there are faint signs that these ideas are emerging in some developing countries. However, if this is the only means of controlling the flow of arms, it will certainly take a very long time.

> There must be a way of coming down the hill, of de-escalating . . . the only solution is not to give us more arms for our security, but to give us more security so that we can have less arms.
> *General Moshe Dayan, August 1976*

# Glossary

**Adversary**    An enemy or opponent.

**Ally**    A friendly country.

**ANZUS**    A security treaty among Australia, New Zealand and the U.S.

**Apartheid**    South African system of government based on racial segregation.

**Balance of payments**    The difference in value between the goods that a country imports and those that it exports.

**Barter**    Swapping goods instead of paying in cash.

**Civil**    Not military.

**Cold War**    A nonmilitary, nonviolent conflict over ideological beliefs carried out through propaganda and other methods that foster mutual distrust and dislike.

**Commodities**    Goods that can be sold, e.g. sugar, coffee.

**Conference on Disarmament**    United Nations committee responsible for negotiating disarmament.

*Contras*    The antigovernment guerrilla forces in Nicaragua.

**Conventional weapons**    Any weapon that is not a nuclear weapon or a chemical/biological weapon.

**Debt crisis**    The problem of many developing countries owing huge sums of money to Western banks but being unable to pay them back.

**Disarmament**    Abolition or substantial reduction of weapons or military forces.

**Domestic**    To do with things at home or inside a country.

**Embargo**    A law that prevents trade with a certain country.

**Exporter**    A country that sells weapons to another. Sometimes exporters are called suppliers.

**Foreign exchange**    The currency of developed countries, e.g. dollars, sterling (British) and yen (Japanese).

**Foreign policy**    The policy that a country has toward other countries.

**GDP**    Gross Domestic Product. The total value of goods and services produced by a country, usually measured per year.

**General Assembly**    The United Nations decision-making body.

**Guidance system**    The part of a missile that guides it to its target.

**Importer**    A country that buys weapons from another. Importers are sometimes called recipients.

**League of Nations**    International organization established after World War I to perform a role similar to that of the United Nations.

**Military balance**    A comparison of the numbers of weapons possessed by two enemies; e.g., India and Pakistan, or NATO and the Warsaw Pact.

**Military coup**    When the armed forces take over the government of a country.

**Military government**    Government by the armed forces.

**National security**    A country's security.

**NATO**    The North Atlantic Treaty Organization. The military alliance that is made up of Belgium, Britain, Canada, Greece, Iceland, Italy, Luxembourg, the Netherlands, Norway, Portugal, Spain, Turkey, the United States and West Germany.

**Revolution**    The overthrow of a government by force.

**SALT**    Strategic Arms Limitation Treaty. A treaty signed by the United States and the Soviet Union that limits the number of their nuclear weapons.

**SIPRI**    The Stockholm International Peace Research Institute. A peace research organization funded by the Swedish government.

**Superpowers**    The U.S. and the Soviet Union.

**Turnover**    The total sales of a company.

**United Nations**    International organization established after World War II to foster agreement among nations, particularly in relation to development and disarmament.

**Volatile**    Something that changes very quickly and suddenly.

**Warsaw Pact**    The Warsaw Treaty Organization. The military alliance that is made up of Bulgaria, Czechoslovakia, East Germany, Hungary, Poland, Romania and the Soviet Union.

# Books to read

The Cold War by John Pimlott (Watts, 1987)

The Nuclear Freeze Movement by Judith Bentley (Watts, 1984)

National Defense Spending: How Much Is Enough? by David Olmos (Watts, 1984)

The Nuclear Arms Race by L. B. Taylor (Watts, 1982)

The Arms Race and Arms Control by Richard Smoke (Walker, 1988)

The Nuclear Arms Race: Can We Survive It? by Ann E. Weiss (Houghton Mifflin, 1983)

# Further information

You can contact these organizations to find out more about some of the subjects covered in this book.

Arms Control and Disarmament Agency (ACDA)
Washington, D.C. 20451

Peace Education Resources
1501 Cherry Street
Philadelphia, PA 19102

Stockholm International Peace Research Institute (SIPRI)
Bergshama S-171
73 Solna
Sweden

United Nations Center for Disarmament
New York, NY 10017

World Priorities
Box 25140
Washington, D.C. 20007

Committee for National Security
1742 "N" Street, N.W.
Washington, D.C. 20036

# Picture Acknowledgments

The pictures in this book were supplied by the following: Associated Press 9; Camera Press 26, 33; Alan Hutchison 11, 29, 32; Rex Features cover, frontispiece, 20, 21, 22, 27, 28, 38, 39, 41; Topham Picture Library 6, 13, 37, 42; TRH 10, 12, 14, 15, 18, 19, 23, 24, 25, 40; Wayland 31; Zefa 36. The artwork on page 7, 16, 17 and 35 is by Robert Burns.

# Index

The figures in **bold** refer to pictures.